Bootloader Source Code for ATMega168 using STK500
For Microsoft Windows
Including Makefile and Test Program

First Edition

Herb Norbom

Author of:
Robot Wireless Control Made Simple with Python and C
Python Version 2.6 Introduction using IDLE
Python Version 2.7 Introduction using IDLE
Python Version 3.2 Introduction using IDLE and PythonWin

Where we are aware of a trademark that name has been printed with a Capital Letter.

Great care has been taken to provide accurate information, by both the author and the publisher, no expressed or implied warranty of any kind is given. No liability is assumed for any damages in connection with any information provided.

Table of Contents

PREFACE

A large part of this project is on how to configure and load programs on to an ATMega168 microchip. I am going into some depth on the 'BOOTLOADER'. The complete source code for the bootloader.c, testAVRlib.c and uart.c are included. The 'Makefile' for each program is included. For our bootloader we need to have a device to load that software, I will be using an STK500. This project is aimed at readers running Microsoft Windows.

In this project we will start with a microchip that does not have a bootloader or bootstrap on it. We will spend some time looking at and burning the fuses and lock bits for the AtMega168. We will be writing a bootloader program for the chip. We will build a library for our common function. We will progress to writing our application test program code and loading it on to the microchip. One of my goals is to give you the knowledge to become as independent as possible from suppliers. I will be using open source or otherwise free software. We will be using Atmel microchip's and when possible Atmel software. As a point of reference I am currently running Microsoft Windows XP Professional Version 2002 Service Pack 3 on a Dell Dimension with Pentium4 CPU 3.00GHz.

PROCESS STEPS

- Of course you need the hardware, chips, ISP device, misc. parts, etc.
- You need the software for the programs 'WinAvr-2010.
- You need to setup your directories.
- Build your breadboards for programing the chip (We will build two).
- You need to burn the fuses and lock bits (optional if you are buying chips with bootloader installed.)
- You need to write and load your bootloader.c program, including writing the Makefile. (Optional if included on your chip.)
- Build a library for storing the UART common files.
- We will write a small test program to test your bootloader, you will write another Makefile for loading the test program to your microchip.

Supplies And Devices

Unless you have programed microchips before you are going to need some devices and some parts. Our chips do not have a bootloader installed. To set the fuses on the chips you are going to need a chip programmer or In-System-Programer(ISP). We are going to be working with the Atmel chip called the Atmega168. The following list gives you a complete parts list, substitute as you like.

Part	Possible Source	Source Part #	Min Qty	Approx. Price	Ext. Price
Atmega168-20PU	Mouser Electronics	556-ATMEGA168-20PU	1	3.11	3.11
Linear Regulator-5V	Mouser Electronics	511-L7805CV	2	0.59	1.18
Crystal 14.7456	Mouser Electronics	695-HC49US-147-U	2	0.52	1.04
Capacitor 104 0.1uF	Electronix Express	14DK050.01U	2	0.10	0.20
Capacitor of approx 220uf 35V	Electronix Express	14ER035220U	2	0.15	0.30
Resistor Kit –for selection	Electronix Express	13RK7305	1	11.95	11.95

Part	Possible Source	Source Part #	Min Qty	Approx. Price	Ext. Price
Half-Size Bread Board	AdaFruit	ID:64	2	5.00	10.00
Hook Up Wire 22AWG solid core	get best price	you do not need a lot for this project			
Breadboard-friendly SPDT Slide Switch	AdaFruit	ID: 805	1	1.95	1.95
USB to TTL Serial Cable	AdaFruit	ID: 954	1	9.95	9.95
AVR STK500 USB ISP Programmer	Sure Electronics	RDB-DA11114	1	22.99	22.99
LED	Mouser Electronics (buy several)	749-5AC BUT there are many to choose from	1	0.30	0.30
ZIF socket 28-pin(optional)	AdaFruit	ID: 382	1	3.00	3.00

For the resistors and capacitors, this project requires only a couple of each. If you are buying from Electronix Express consider the kits, as there is a minimum order limit of $20.00. If you want to burn fuses and load a bootloader you need a device similar to the STK500. There are many of them on the market. For all of the items listed this is a possible parts and POSSIBLE supplier list. For the low priced items you may want to buy several as multiple shipments will end up costing more. While I have used these suppliers I am not saying they are the best or the least expensive. I am not affiliated with any of them.

Windows – C Library and Programmer's Notepad

This software will give you the libraries needed for compiling your C programs and a very nice editor. We are going to need some software tools later, specifically a C compiler with libraries, so I am going to have you get the editor that comes with that package now. Go to http://winavr.sourceforge.net/download.html. Select download and follow the instructions. The version we are using here is WinAvr-2010 and is approximately 28.8Mb. This download includes 'avrdude' and an editor called Programmer's Notepad.

Work Directories

We are going to be writing a number of programs and it can get very confusing where they are located. Also from a backup view point it is nice to have them in a separate directory, probably several. I suggest you make a separate directory now. I called my directory 'HerbKit'. Within HerbKit you are going to need some sub directories. I suggest the following, which we will go into more detail as we progress.

- compileLinkBootloader   For our bootloader.c program and its Makefile
- uploadBootloader   Batch files for chip fuse setting and bootloader program Makefile for installation of bootloader
- herbClib   Uart program, header for our application programs and Makefile
- testAVRlibrary   Test program to make sure all is working and Makefile

Windows-Avrdude

There are a number of methods for running 'avrdude', we are going to use the 'DOS PROMPT or COMMAND WINDOW'. Open a DOS prompt by either pressing the "Windows and r keys" at the same time or by going to start, select run and enter 'cmd'. Note what directory the window opens in. You will probably want to create and go to a work directory. You may want to create a batch file that you can run each time to take you to appropriate directory. Our first directory will be one for keeping our fuse and lock settings used to configure the microchip. I will call my directory 'uploadBootloader'.

The bat file I made is shown in the following. (I will mark the beginning and end of files with START** and END** statements, do not include in your files.

```
START BATCH FILE**
REM stk500work.bat
REM  Herb Norbom 8/7/2013
cd my documents\herbkit\uploadbootloader
dir
END**
```

I made the file using the Programmer's Notepad.EXE, I suggest you set up a shortcut to the program. Make sure you save the bat file to the same directory your DOS prompt opens in, or have it in an appropriate search path.

We need to make sure the appropriate program for writing to the microchip is available. Type 'avrdude' and press enter. This should give you all the options for running avrdude. If it does not I would guess that 'winavr-20100110' did not make it to your search path. Type 'path' and see if it is there? Note if installation went okay it should have added it for you. You may want to try logout/login or rebooting if having problems.

STK500 SETUP

If you are using a device similar to the STK500 your set up may be similar, but the following description is for the STK500 purchased from Sure Electronics. The first item is to build out our breadboard. Take your time. I have set my board up to have the microchip's pin 1 in position 1 on the breadboard. This works great for the left side, but doesn't help with the right side as you can see in the diagram. Hopefully you are familiar with the breadboard, but if not you will quickly figure out that the left and right half of the board are not connected, unless you connect them. If you look at the breadboard rows 26 and 27 you see the connections between the positive and negative rails. I am using an outside power source to the breadboard, required by my STK500. I connect the positive power source to the 5V voltage regulator input and the voltage regulator output to the positive rail of the breadboard. The outside power source can be a 9V battery, or in my case an AC/DC converter with 9V DC output. In any event your microchip needs 5V DC.

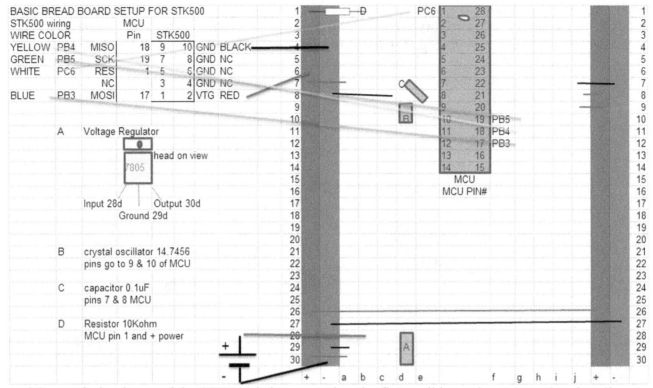

BASIC BREAD BOARD SETUP FOR STK500

STK500 wiring		MCU					
WIRE COLOR		Pin	STK500				
YELLOW	PB4	MISO	18	9	10	GND	BLACK
GREEN	PB5	SCK	19	7	8	GND	NC
WHITE	PC6	RES	1	5	6	GND	NC
		NC		3	4	GND	NC
BLUE	PB3	MOSI	17	1	2	VTG	RED

A   Voltage Regulator

7805   head on view

Input 28d   Output 30d
Ground 29d

B   crystal oscillator 14.7456
pins go to 9 & 10 of MCU

C   capacitor 0.1uF
pins 7 & 8 MCU

D   Resistor 10Kohm
MCU pin 1 and + power

MCU
MCU PIN#

One of the confusing items of the STK500 is in connecting the flat or ribbon wire strip to the pig tail. Remember on a flat or ribbon strip the red wire is for pin 1. Also I am sure you remember that on a connector there is usually some type of indicator as to which pin is 1. On my setup, impossible to see in the picture there is a little arrow shape on both the connectors, that also indicates pin 1, so match them up.

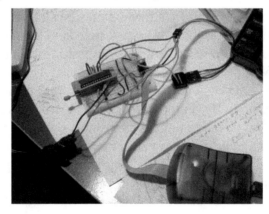

The picture shows an LED, this is optional. I just put it on to remind me when the auxiliary power is on. If you add the LED make sure you also add a resistor. As I found the wiring from the STD500 through the ribbon or flat cable to the 10 pin connector, then to the 6pin connector, then to the breadboard a little confusing I prepared the following exhibit. I hope it helps.

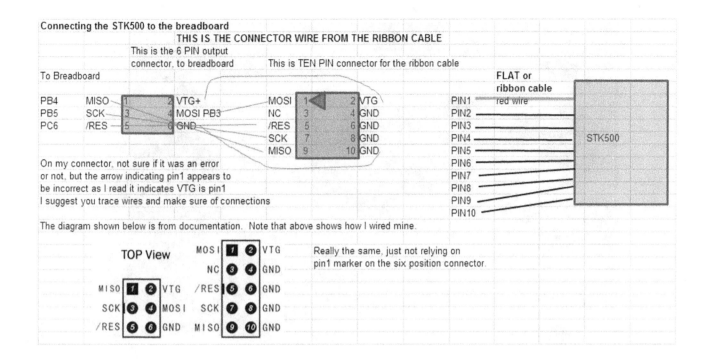

Connecting the STK500 to the breadboard

THIS IS THE CONNECTOR WIRE FROM THE RIBBON CABLE

This is the 6 PIN output connector, to breadboard

This is TEN PIN connector for the ribbon cable

To Breadboard

PB4	MISO	1		2	VTG+
PB5	SCK	3		4	MOSI PB3
PC6	/RES	5		6	GND

MOSI	1		2	VTG
NC	3		4	GND
/RES	5		6	GND
SCK	7		8	GND
MISO	9		10	GND

FLAT or ribbon cable

PIN1	red wire
PIN2	
PIN3	
PIN4	
PIN5	
PIN6	
PIN7	
PIN8	
PIN9	
PIN10	

STK500

On my connector, not sure if it was an error or not, but the arrow indicating pin1 appears to be incorrect as I read it indicates VTG is pin1 I suggest you trace wires and make sure of connections

The diagram shown below is from documentation. Note that above shows how I wired mine.

TOP View

MOSI	1	2	VTG
NC	3	4	GND
/RES	5	6	GND
SCK	7	8	GND
MISO	9	10	GND

MISO	1	2	VTG
SCK	3	4	MOSI
/RES	5	6	GND

Really the same, just not relying on pin1 marker on the six position connector.

Testing Our STK500

You will be plugging the USB cable into your computer. In my case I am using COM7 setup for 115,200 baud, 8 data bits, no parity, 1 stop bit and no flow control. I always have the power off and the USB connector unplugged when I am putting a chip on or taking a chip off the board. Remember static electricity is not your friend, so ground yourself. Remember you may also need to add external power to your breadboard.

Chip in place, USB connected and with external power on. Get to your command prompt execute your bat file to get to your work directory, my file is stk500work.bat.   Type the following on the command line, we are just going to try to read the chip, no writing at this point.

        avrdude -c stk500 -p m168 -P /com7 -b 115200 -v

You should get something very similar to the following, which I broke into several screen shots.

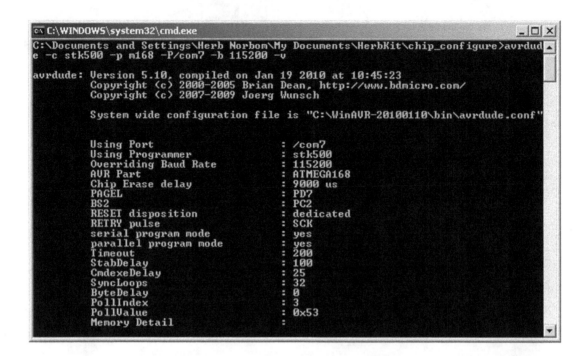

```
C:\WINDOWS\system32\cmd.exe                                    _ | □ | X
C:\Documents and Settings\Herb Norbom\My Documents\HerbKit\chip_configure>avrdud
e -c stk500 -p m168 -P/com7 -b 115200 -v

avrdude: Version 5.10, compiled on Jan 19 2010 at 10:45:23
          Copyright (c) 2000-2005 Brian Dean, http://www.bdmicro.com/
          Copyright (c) 2007-2009 Joerg Wunsch

          System wide configuration file is "C:\WinAVR-20100110\bin\avrdude.conf"

          Using Port                    : /com7
          Using Programmer              : stk500
          Overriding Baud Rate          : 115200
          AVR Part                      : ATMEGA168
          Chip Erase delay              : 9000 us
          PAGEL                         : PD7
          BS2                           : PC2
          RESET disposition             : dedicated
          RETRY pulse                   : SCK
          serial program mode           : yes
          parallel program mode         : yes
          Timeout                       : 200
          StabDelay                     : 100
          CmdexeDelay                   : 25
          SyncLoops                     : 32
          ByteDelay                     : 0
          PollIndex                     : 3
          PollValue                     : 0x53
          Memory Detail                 :
```

```
C:\WINDOWS\system32\cmd.exe                                    _ | □ | X
                                     Block Poll           Page
       Polled
            Memory Type Mode Delay Size  Indx Paged  Size  Size #Pages MinW  Max
W   ReadBack
___  _____  ____ ____ ____ ____ ____ _____ _____ _____ _____ _____ _____

            eeprom      65    5    4    0 no     512    4     0  3600   36
00 0xff 0xff
            flash       65    6  128    0 yes  16384  128   128  4500   45
00 0xff 0xff
            lfuse        0    0    0    0 no       1    0     0  4500   45
00 0x00 0x00
            hfuse        0    0    0    0 no       1    0     0  4500   45
00 0x00 0x00
            efuse        0    0    0    0 no       1    0     0  4500   45
00 0x00 0x00
            lock         0    0    0    0 no       1    0     0  4500   45
00 0x00 0x00
            calibration  0    0    0    0 no       1    0     0     0
 0 0x00 0x00
            signature    0    0    0    0 no       3    0     0     0
 0 0x00 0x00
```

```
C:\WINDOWS\system32\cmd.exe                                    _|□|×
          Programmer Type : STK500U2
          Description     : Atmel STK500
          Programmer Model: AVRISP
          Hardware Version: 15
          Firmware Version Master : 2.10
          Vtarget         : 0.0 U
          SCK period      : 129.2 us

avrdude: AUR device initialized and ready to accept instructions

Reading | ################################################### | 100% 0.05s

avrdude: Device signature = 0x1e9406
avrdude: safemode: lfuse reads as F7
avrdude: safemode: hfuse reads as D5
avrdude: safemode: efuse reads as 0
avrdude: current erase-rewrite cycle count is -256 (if being tracked)

avrdude: safemode: lfuse reads as F7
avrdude: safemode: hfuse reads as D5
avrdude: safemode: efuse reads as 0
avrdude: safemode: Fuses OK

avrdude done.  Thank you.
```

The above setting were not for a new 'raw' chip but from one I have programed previously. The key elements we are looking for at this stage are the fuse settings and the Device Signature. Before we get to far into this you need to recognize that the values shown for lfuse, hfuse, and efuse are hex values. I suggest you check on the web and find a site for converting hex to decimal. I am going to prepare a table that breaks down the fuses into their individual bit names. I will also show what the settings are for a new 'raw' chip and for what setting I want for my chip. Review the Datasheet for the ATmega168 under Boot Loader Support to check what I am suggesting. With the Atmega168 there are a number of chips. The important point is that the Device Signature we use in our program and Makefile must agree with the microchip's signature. The plain Atmega168 has a Device Signature of 0x1e9406 as shown in the example. There is also a Atmega168p and it has a Device Signature of 0x1e940b. You will need to adjust accordingly if using the Atmega168p.

SETTING THE FUSES AND LOCK

Other than potentially destroying your chip this section is relatively straight forward. Be careful, double check your work and verify the instructions I give you with the Datasheet. Remember if you purchased chips that have the bootloader installed you may be able to skip this section. If you haven't been looking at the Datasheet now is the time, get familiar, page references are to the Datasheet. We will be configuring our chips to include the following items:

- Use full size of Boot Loader Section
- Preserve EEPROM memory through Chip Erase
- Set Brown Out level MinV=2.5V
- Divide clock by 8
- Full Swing Crystal Oscillator (see page 32, section 8.4)
- Do not allow SPM to write to the Boot Loader Section.

Be sure you are working with an ATmega168 that has the Device Signature 0x1e9406, see page 289.

You can put the fuse commands in a batch file and execute it to do all the fuses and lock at one pass. I generally burn the fuses with the assistance of a Makefile, which I will detail at the end of the section. I am going to go through each fuse, please follow along using the Datasheet. One of the many items that you may find confusing is that the value of '1' means the byte is unprogrammed. One more point of confusion deals with setting that are 'not used'. The documentation says that the setting is a '1'. You will notice on a new chip that the setting is a '0'. If you try to set a 'not used' Byte to a '1' chances are it will not be accepted. I am sure you are going to have more questions about avrdude. The documentation is I believe automatically included with the windows version, in my case installed at C:\WinAVR-20100110\doc\avrdude.

I hope you found a site to assist you in converting the hex value to binary. The avrdude display shows the fuse settings in hex, but to understand the setting you need to convert to binary. Of course when burning the fuse you will need to use a hex value. Writing fuses and lock bits are a complex subject and you need to be warned that you can fry or 'brick' your microchip, so be careful.

Extended Fuse Byte

Let's start with the 'EFuse', see page 275 for BOOTRST and 288

	Extended Fuse Byte	Bit No	Default	Mouser	HerbKit	References
	not used	7	1	0	0	
	not used	6	1	0	0	
	not used	5	1	0	0	
	not used	4	1	0	0	
	not used	3	1	0	0	
BOOTSZ1	Select Boot Size	2	0	0	0	page 288, Table 27-5
BOOTSZ0	Select Boot Size	1	0	0	0	page 288, Table 27-5
BOOTRST	Select Reset Vector	0	1	1	0	page 275, Table 26-4
	HEX VALUE		F9	1	0	

Let's read the Fuse values and get used to the avrdude commands and displays. Type the following command to display the current settings.
avrdude -c STK500 -p m168 -P com7 -v

To burn the efuse the command is: avrdude -c STK500 -p m168 -P com7 -b 115200 -U efuse:w:0x00:m
Run the display command and make sure that the fuse value changed.

High Fuse Byte

'HFuse', see page 288

	Fuse HIGH Byte	Bit No	Default	Mouser	HerbKit	References
RSTDISBL	External Reset Disable	7	1	1	1	
DWEN	debug WIRE enable	6	1	1	1	
SPIEN	Enable Serial Program and Data Downloading	5	0	0	0	not accessible in serial programming
WDTON	Watchdog timer Always On	4	1	1	1	see page 54
EESAVE	EEPROM memory is preserved through the	3	1	1	0	want to preserve EEPROM memory

	Chip Erase					
BODLEVEL2	Brown-out Detector trigger level	2	1	1	1	page 288, Table 27-5
BODLEVEL1	Brown-out Detector trigger level	1	1	1	0	page 288, Table 27-5
BODLEVEL0	Brown-out Detector trigger level	0	1	1	1	page 275, Table 26-4
	HEX VALUE		DF	DF	D5	

To burn the hfuse the command is:
avrdude -c STK500 -p m168 -P com7 -b 115200 -U hfuse:w:0xd5:m

Run the display command and make sure that the fuse value changed.
avrdude -c STK500 -p m168 -P com7 -v

Low Fuse Byte

'LFuse', see page 289 Table 27-7

	Fuse LOW Byte	Bit No	Default	Mouser	HerbKit	References
CKDIV8	Divide clock by 8	7	0	0	1	we want to divide by 8
CKOUT	clock output	6	1	1	1	not using
SUT1	Select start-up time	5	1	1	1	Table 8-9 page 35
SUT0	Select start-up time	4	0	0	1	Table 8-9 page 35
CKSEL3	Select Clock Source	3	0	0	0	Table 8-8 page 35
CKSEL2	Select Clock Source	2	0	0	1	
CKSEL1	Select Clock Source	1	1	1	1	
CKSEL0	Select Clock Source	0	0	0	1	
	HEX VALUE		62	62	F7	

To burn the lfuse the command is:
avrdude -c STK500 -p m168 -P com7 -b 115200 -U lfuse:w:0xf7:m
Run the display command and make sure that the fuse value changed.
avrdude -c STK500 -p m168 -P com7 -v

Lock Bit Byte

'Lock Bit Byte', see page 273 Section 26.5 **Remember '1' means unprogrammed**

	Fuse LOW Byte	Bit No	Default	Mouser	HerbKit	References
	not used	7	1	0	0	
	not used	6	1	0	0	
BLB12	Boot Lock bit	5	1	1	1	see page274,table 26-3

BLB11	Boot Lock bit	4	1	1	0	see page274,table 26-3
BLB02	Boot Lock bit	3	1	1	1	see page274,table 26-2
BLB01	Boot Lock bit	2	1	1	1	see page274,table 26-2
LB2	Lock Bit	1	1	1	1	see page286,table 27-2
LB1	Lock Bit	0	1	1	1	see page286,table 27-2
	HEX VALUE		FF	3F	2F	
	Based on above BLB0 MODE	MODE	1	1	1	
	Based on above BLB1 MODE	MODE	1	1	2	

BLB0 MODE=1	No restrictions for SPM or LPM accessing the Application section.
BLB1 MODE=1	No restrictions for SPM or LPM accessing the Boot Loader section.
BLB1 MODE=2	SPM is not allowed to write to the Boot Loader section.

The lock bits are just a little bit more complicated to view. We will write them to a text file and view them with our Programmer's Notepad, or what ever text editor you like. We want to look at the current settings prior to making any changes. The command for this is:

    avrdude -c STK500 -p m168 -P com7 -b 115200 -U lock:r:fuse_lock:h

(Note the above command is one line, but if you want to continue a command on a new line enter a backslash and you will see a > displayed for you to continue your command.)

We are writing the fuse settings to a file named 'fuse_lock' in our current directory. You can use any name you like for the file. As a side note you can use the same technique to write the fuse settings to individual files.

To burn the lock bits the command is:
avrdude -c STK500 -p m168 -P com7 -b 115200 -U lock:w:0x2f:m

To check, run the command to write the lock settings to the file, make sure that the lock settings changed.

Batch file to burn FUSES

I like to have a batch file for writing the fuse settings. I have two files as I have sometimes had trouble setting the lock and fuses in one file. Later on I will give you my Makefile which has all the commands for the fuses, lock and installation of our application program. I saved the this batch file in the 'uploadBootlloader' directory the first batch file is named 'STK500write168Fuses.bat'.

BATCH FILE TO BURN FUSES**

rem display setting fuses
avrdude -c STK500 -p m168 -P com7 -b 115200 -v
rem should get Device Signature= 0x1e9406
rem EFUSE
avrdude -c STK500 -p m168 -P com7 -b 115200 -U efuse:w:0x0:m
rem HFUSE
avrdude -c STK500 -p m168 -P /com7 -b 115200 -U hfuse:w:0xd5:m

rem LFUSE

avrdude -c STK500 -p m168 -P /com7 -b 115200 -U lfuse:w:0xf7:m

END BATCH FILE**

Batch file to burn LOCK BYTES

A separate batch file from the fuses. The lock byte hex value is written. You can look at the output displayed to verify the new setting or run command to write the 'fuse_lock' setting to the file. I saved the this batch file in the 'uploadBootlloader' directory the second batch file is named 'STK500write168lock.bat'.

BATCH FILE TO BURN LOCK BITS**

rem write LOCK BYTES atmega168 using STK500

avrdude -c STK500 -p m168 -P com7 -b 115200 -U lock:w:0x2f:m

rem should get Device Signature= 0x1e9406

END BATCH FILE**

BOOTLOADER

Our microchip needs to have a 'bootstrap' or 'bootloader'. Before getting into the bootloader it may help you to understand the concept, think of it as just another program. We will write ours in 'C'. In the very simplest terms this is a program that the microchip executes as it starts or 'boots' and instructs the program to run the application or load a new program. While this program is just another program it does have some specific abilities as it needs to set up the hardware. This program needs to be placed in a specific section or position within the microchip's memory called the Boot Loader Section or 'BLS'. The BLS resides in the flash memory. I hope you see in the Datasheet that the flash memory is or can be divided into two sections, the BLS and Application sections. This is a complex subject and you need to be warned that you can fry or 'brick' your microchip, so be careful.

BOOTLOADER PROGRAM

Now that you are somewhat comfortable with the STK500 and avrdude we will move into the meat of the book. We are going to write a bootloader program using avr-gcc and the 'C' programming language. You hopefully downloaded the documentation and examples, for windows. mine is located in C:\WinAVR-20100110\doc\avr-libc. We will also cover the Makefile, some documentation is located in C:\WinAVR-20100110\mfile.

You may have found the various bootloader examples out on the web to be very complex and generally missing a key piece of the pie. There are a number of free bootloader.hex files available on the web. But, if you are here you are like me, and want to know how it works.

We are going to write a bootloader.c program that is specific for the Atmega168 and the ISP STK500. To keep this solution as simple as possible, we are writing code for one chip and one ISP. I have used standard header files, no auxiliary configuration or header files. While the program will use UART, I have included that start-up or 'init' settings in the program to avoid having another level of confusion.

At this point I would hope that you have a general working knowledge of the "C" programing language, and a handle on the text editor, I will be using Programmer's Notepad. I am going to provide some discussion first and then the complete program source code. Within the source code I have added comments to assist us in understanding what we are trying to do. Leave the comments out or modify as you like.

I suggest that you open your program editor and type the following comments to get a program started.

Remember in "C" comments begin with a // or you can do the block comments. For this book I am marking the start and end of the program with START** and END**. Don't include the markers with your code.

START**

//Bootloader for ATmega168 uses AVR109 and AVR910 protocols
//Herb at RyMax, Inc. 8/19/2013
//this program will always run first, decision made based on PB0(high or low)
//on loading new program or running application

END**

Save your program with the name bootloader.c, type of C/C++, in the directory 'compileLinkBootloader' or whatever directory you want to designate.

Include Headers

Next we need to talk a little about the header files we want our program to include. As I said we are going to use standard header files that are included with avr. It is worthwhile to know where they are, you can open them with your editor. I strongly advise that you DO NOT CHANGE any of them, just look if you like. The files are located on my windows computer at: C:\WinAVR-20100110\avr\include\avr. These files save you a tremendous amount of work. The first one we are going to include is <avr/io.h>. By including this header file you begin the definition of our microchip. This file gives us access to our specific microchip, which we will later define in our Makefile as 'atmega168' or m168 using the avrdude commands.(Much more on that latter). We are going to need the following headers, some defines, some work variables and the section where the 'code' is written. Add the following to the end of your program, and save the program. (At the of the section are screen shots of the entire bootloader.c program.)

START**

```
// the includes are in dir C:\WinAVR-20100110\avr\include\avr\
#include <avr/io.h>    //includes sfr_defs, portpins, common, version
//above also selects ioM168.h,WHICH INTURN LOADS iomx8.h
//portpins defines the PORTs, direction, pins, registers, etc.
#include <avr/boot.h>//turns off interrupts, SPM Control, Fuse bits, & more
#include <avr/eeprom.h>
#include <avr/pgmspace.h>
#include <util/delay.h>
//see Atmel .com/images/doc2568.pdf for information on AVR910
#define _AVR910_DEVCODE 0x35
uint16_t flash_loc ;    // flash use byte address
uint16_t eeprom_loc;    // eeprom use byte address
uint16_t temp_loc;          //temp holder
//use the noinline attribute to save bytes
//use static to reduce size, see AVR4027,doc8453.pdf
#define noinline __attribute__((noinline))
int main(void){
//we are going to be entering code here, make sure you do not lose the '} 'at the end as we add code.
}
```
END**

We now have enough of a program to write our Makefile and test the very basics. Generally there are a number of assigns done in the Makefile. For example, setting a variable name for baud rate, and assigning the baud rate to the variable at the beginning of the file. We are going to make this a very specific Makefile and try to avoid the variables. As we are learning I think this is easier. The goal for this Makefile is to compile our bootloader.c program, link the program as needed, produce an object file and a hex file. We are going to include some list files just to help you get familiar with them but they will not be needed for our steps here. Our Makefile will include the start position for the BOOT LOADER SECTION as defined by our fuse settings. While our bootloader.c program is just getting started I want to develop a complete Makefile for the purposes described above. The actual uploading of our hex program file will be covered later.

Makefile-compile

Open your text editor, and create a new file. If you are using the Programmer's NotePad , the type will be 'Make'. Your filename will be 'Makefile' and you will save the file in the same directory as your bootloader.c program. Some general notes on Makefiles are appropriate. A comment is made with a '#' sign, this only applies to the beginning of the line. In our commands that we want to continue on a new line, end the line to be continued with a '\' backslash. While you can have multiple Makefiles in a directory you must be careful of the names and your actual command to start the Make process is slightly different. To keep our programs and actions separate and somewhat simple we will only have one Makefile per directory. There is additional documentation in C:\WinAVR-20100110\doc\avr-libc.

I am going to list the entire Makefile for compiling, linking and generating support files in the following. I have included descriptions that you should not enter in your Makefile.

		DESCRIPTIONS DO NOT INCLUDE IN Makefile
# Makefile for bootloader		The # means this is a comment line.
all: compile		What we are processing with the make file. If just make is typed on command line will do all sections. If we type 'make compile', will just do that one section
compile:		Section defined.
avr-gcc\	-g\	We are using the avr-gcc compilier, -g for producing debugging information. Note the '\' means the command continued on next line.
	-Os\	Optimize for size.
	-mmcu=atmega168\	Specify the ATMEL AVR defined
	-DF_CPU=14745600\	Two things, the '-D' defines a name, also setting the clock speed
	-std=gnu99\	Set the language standard, we are using gnu
	-DBOOT_SECTION_START=0x3800\	Two things, the '-D' defines a name, also giving hex value for start of boot section
	-Werror\	Make all warnings into errors
	-Wl,--section-start=.text=0X3800\	Linking, Wl (note this is a small letter L, not a '1'). Passing the item after the comma to the linker.
	-o bootloader.o bootloader.c	Produce an output file named bootloader.o
avr-objcopy -j .text -O ihex bootloader.o bootloader.hex		Copy the bootloader.o file to the bootloader.hex file and use the library to change to the desired format
avr-objcopy -j .text -O ihex bootloader.hex bootloader.lss		Copy the bootloader.o file to the bootloader.lss file and use the library to change to the desired format
avr-objdump -S bootloader.o > bootloader.lst		Displays information about the bootloader.o in the bootloader.lst file.
@echo "*********"		Simple echo to print the stars
@echo "compiled for: atmega168"		Simple echo saying what is in the " "
@echo -n "bootloader size is: "		Simple echo saying what is in the " ", note it starts with -n which generates a new line.
@echo		Simple echo to print a blank line
@avr-size bootloader.hex		Displays size stats of hex file, uses the default format.
@echo "*********"		Simple echo to print the stars

You can have other sections than the 'compile:' included in your Makefile. Some people like to add a 'clean:' section to remove files, pursue other sections as you like. In a later Makefile we will have some additional sections.

BOOT_SECTION_START

I hope that the descriptions with the Makefile are adequate, but I know we need to talk some more about the start of the BOOT_SECTION_START. This can be confusing. First remember how we defined our fuses. We defined a boot section size of 1,024. Look back at the EFuse and the Datasheet page 283, Table 26-9. It is important to note that the 1,024 is words and not bytes. Our ATMega168 uses two bytes for every word. So our boot size is 2,048 bytes. The chip memory is organized with the Boot Section at the top of the flash memory. Our total flash memory is 16,384 bytes. The Datasheet, page 283, shows that for our 1,024 Boot Size, the Start-Boot-Loader-Section is 0x1C00. That hex value in decimal is 7,168. Now remember we are talking about 'words', to convert the 7,168 words to bytes we multiply by two and get 14,336 bytes. With our flash section ending at 16,384 bytes and the boot-section at the top of the flash section to get the start position we subtract 2,048 bytes from our total bytes of 16,384. This gives us a byte boot start of 14,336, which checks with our previously calculated boot start section. Of course, not quite done as we need to give the start position in hex format. So we convert the 14,336 bytes to hex and get 0x3800. If you play with the Datasheet and the memory definitions I think it all will fall into place.

Some other facts that may help are from page290, Table 27.5 with some math added.

WORD -bytes	PAGE-words	PAGE-bytes	No. of pages	FLASH size -bytes
2	64	128	128	16,384
given	given	2 x 64 = 128	given	64 x 128 x 2 =16,384

First Compile of bootloader.c

Open a DOS or command prompt window and change to the 'compileLinkBootloader' directory. This directory needs to have our bootloader.c program and our Makefile. Type 'make' and press return. If all is well this will be your display. Notice that all the commands are displayed.

```
C:\WINDOWS\system32\cmd.exe                                          _ |□| X|

C:\Documents and Settings\Herb Norbom\My Documents\HerbKit\compileLinkBootloader
>make
avr-gcc -g\
            -Os\
            -mmcu=atmega168\
            -DF_CPU=14745600\
            -std=gnu99\
            -DBOOT_SECTION_START=0x3800\
            -Werror\
            -Wl,--section-start=.text=0X3800\
            -o bootloader.o bootloader.c
avr-objcopy -j .text -O ihex bootloader.o bootloader.hex
avr-objcopy -j .text -O ihex bootloader.hex bootloader.lss
avr-objdump -S bootloader.o > bootloader.lst
*********
compiled for: atmega168
bootloader size is:
    text    data     bss     dec     hex filename
       0     154       0     154      9a bootloader.hex
*********

C:\Documents and Settings\Herb Norbom\My Documents\HerbKit\compileLinkBootloader
>
```

After you successfully run this, look in your directory and you should see the additional files. You can use your Programmer's Notepad or other text editor to view the bootloader.lss and bootloader.lst files. These files are about memory locations, mainly of use if you are having problems with your programs.

Bootloader – Communication Uart

In an attempt to keep this program as simple as possible we are putting the code for uart communication into our program rather than into separate header files. This section deals with putting characters and strings; getting characters; and defining our communication protocols. If you are following with the Datasheet look at the registers and you will get a feel for how the communication flow is controlled. For the protocols all that we need to set up in this program is the 'get' and 'put' functions, baud rate and the enabling of the transmit and receive procedures. Add this code just before the start of the 'int main(void) section.

START**

```
//output character
static noinline void uart_putc(uint8_t data)
```

```
    {   // loop until all data transmitted  see page 191
  while ((UCSR0A & (1<<UDRE0))==0);//if UDRE0=1 buffer empty & ready
    // put data in buffer
    UDR0 = data;}
//output string
static inline void uart_puts(uint8_t buffer[])
        {   // send until end of string
  while (*buffer != 0) {
    uart_putc(*buffer);
    buffer++;}}
//read character
static noinline uint8_t uart_getc(void)
        {   // wait for character to be received
        while (!(UCSR0A & (1<<RXC0)));
  /* return received byte */
  return UDR0;}
//init the hardware uart
static inline void init_uart(void)
        {   // set baud rate for 115,200 using F_CPU =14745600
        UBRR0H = 0;
        UBRR0L = 7;          //see page 198 set 115,200 baud
        UCSR0B = (1<<RXEN0)|(1<<TXEN0);//enable Receiver & Transmitter,pages 192-193
        UCSR0C = (1<<UCSZ01)|(1<<UCSZ00);} //see page 194 set for 8 bit
```

END**

After the 'int main(void) we need to add some variables and a call to our uart function. Add the following 3 lines of code, notice they are indented one tab stop.

START*

```
  uint8_t memory_type;
  uint16_t buffer_size;
  init_uart();
```

END**

In the code we just added we set up registers that turn on and off various features for USART, our serial protocol. I have selected 115200 as our desired BAUD rate. This gives a very low error rate for the crystal oscillator we are using, and it is relatively fast. Our crystal frequency is 14.7456 MHz's. Based on page 198, Table 19-11, we want to set the UBRRn register at 7. (We are using U2Xn =0, of the UCSRnA register that has an Initial Value of 0. See page 191 of Datasheet. We are not going to bother with setup of U2Xn, just know we are using it.)

After you have saved your program run the 'make' command again, after correcting any errors we will move on.

BOOT Load New or Run Existing

With our next section of code we want to be able to tell if our bootloader.c program should run a previously loaded application or if new application software is going to be loaded. With the ATmega168 pulling the PINB to ground, (using our switch or ground wire). Note, when we are ready to load our application program we will be using a different breadboard, described later. If pulled to ground we will want to load new application software if not pulled to ground we will run the existing application. We need to setup the PORT DATA REGISTERS for input and pullup. We also built in a delay to allow the chip registers setup to be completed. Add the following code after the 'init_uart(); statement. Use the same one tab indent.

START**

```
    DDRB &= ~(1<<PB0); //PORT DATA REGISTER set as input
    PORTB |= (1<<PB0); //PORT DATA REGISTER enable pullup
    // wait a little
    _delay_loop_1(200);//arbitrary number
```

END**

After you have saved your program run the 'make' command again, after correcting any errors we will move on.

Decision Time

In this section we will actually test the PINB and run sections of the code for either running the existing application or loading new application software. If PINB is pulled to ground with our switch we will go to the 'start_bootloader' section of code. If not pulled to ground we will jump to our application start address. Add the next section of code after the delayloop_1(200); statement, continue using the same one tab indent.

START**

```
   // bootloader test to see if new program to load
        if(PINB == 0) {//if PINB is pulled to ground
      goto start_bootloader;
    } else { //start application
      // see DataSheet page 65, jump to application program start of flash memory
      MCUCR = 0;
      asm("jmp 0000");}
start_bootloader:    // main communication loop with avrdude

    while (1)

    {   //these are commands from avrdude also look at AVR109 Protocol doc1644.pdf
```

//don't lose '}' at end of this section, should now have two of them at the end of your program.

```
    }
```

END**

After you have saved your program run the 'make' command again, after correcting any errors we will move on.

Communication with avrdude and STK500

This next section of code is the meat of the bootloader program. Here there is communication between our program and our soon to be created new Makefile for the uploading of the application program, not this bootloader program that we are working on now. In this section we will receive input from avrdude and respond accordingly. We will use the 'switch' and 'case' operations. I have tried to put comments in to help you find additional information. (At the end of this section I will show the entire completed program.) Enter the following code after the comment in the 'while (1) ' section. Don't lose the end of section markers '}'.

START**

```c
uint8_t avrdude_cmd = uart_getc();
switch (avrdude_cmd){
    case 'P':  //Enter Programming Mode
            uart_putc('\r');
            break;
    case 'L':  //Leave Programming Mode
            uart_putc('\r');
            break;
    case 'a':  //Auto Increment Address
            uart_putc('Y');
            break;
    case 'A':  //Start address, we want to start at byte 0, but it
            //looks like avrdude needs us to read the address
            //so read and ignore
            temp_loc = (uart_getc() << 8) | uart_getc();
            eeprom_loc = 0;         //set to zero
            flash_loc = 0;          //set to zero
            uart_putc('\r');
            break;
    case 'e':  //Chip Erase, all pages in flash, as per lock-bits
            //bootloader section should be protected by lock-bits
            for (flash_loc = 0; flash_loc < BOOT_SECTION_START;
                    flash_loc += SPM_PAGESIZE) {
                    boot_page_erase_safe(flash_loc);}
            uart_putc('\r');
            break;
    case 'T':  // Select Device Type: received device type
            uart_getc();
            uart_putc('\r');
            break;
    case 's': // Read Signature Bytes: send the signature bytes for this MCU
            uart_putc(SIGNATURE_2); //FROM iom168.h see Datasheet page 289 27.3
            uart_putc(SIGNATURE_1);
            uart_putc(SIGNATURE_0);
            break;
    case 't':  // Return Supported Device Codes, terminate with a nullbyte
            uart_putc(_AVR910_DEVCODE);
            uart_putc(0);
            break;
    case 'S':  // Return Software Identifier, send s[7]
            uart_puts((uint8_t *)"RyMax");
    case 'p':  // Return Programmer Type, 'S' for serial
            uart_putc('S');
            break;
    case 'E':  // Exit Bootloader
            uart_putc('\r');
            break;
    case 'b':  // Check Block Support: return yes, another byte + block size
            uart_putc('Y');
```

```c
                uart_putc(0);
                uart_putc(SPM_PAGESIZE);
                break;
    case 'B':   // Start Block Flash Load, read buffer size (in bytes)
            buffer_size = (uart_getc() << 8) | uart_getc();
            // check buffer size not exceeded
            if (buffer_size > SPM_PAGESIZE) {
                    uart_putc('?');
                    break;}
            //read flash ('F') or eeprom ('E') memory type
            memory_type = uart_getc();
            if (memory_type == 'F'){
                    uint16_t i;
                    uint16_t temp_word_buffer;
                    if (flash_loc > BOOT_SECTION_START) {
                            uart_putc(0);}
                    uint16_t temp_address = flash_loc;
                    boot_spm_busy_wait();
                    // read data, wordwise, low byte first
                    for (i = 0; i < buffer_size/2; i++) {
                            // get data word
                            temp_word_buffer = uart_getc() | (uart_getc() << 8);
                            // write data to temporary buffer
                            boot_page_fill(temp_address, temp_word_buffer);
                            // increment by two, since temp_address is a byte
                            // address, but we are writing words!
                            temp_address += 2;}
                    // after filling the temp buffer, write the page
                    boot_page_write_safe(flash_loc);
                    boot_spm_busy_wait();
                    // re-enable application flash section for read
                    boot_rww_enable();
                    // store next page's address, since auto-address-incrementing
                    flash_loc = temp_address;
                    uart_putc('\r');
        }
        else if (memory_type == 'E'){
            uint8_t temp_data;
            uint16_t i;
            for (i = 0; i < buffer_size; i++) {
                    temp_data = uart_getc();
                    eeprom_write_byte( (uint8_t *)eeprom_loc, temp_data);
                            eeprom_loc++;}
            uart_putc('\r');
            }
            else {uart_putc('?');}
        break;
    case 'g':   // Start Block Flash Read, read byte counter
        buffer_size = (uart_getc() << 8) | uart_getc();
```

```c
    // then, read memory type
    memory_type = uart_getc();
    // memory type is flash
    if (memory_type == 'F')
        { // read buffer_size words
        uint16_t i;
        for (i = 0; i < buffer_size; i += 2) {
                uint16_t temp_word_buffer;  //define 16 bit for word size
                // read word
                temp_word_buffer = pgm_read_word(flash_loc);
                // send data as word
                uart_putc(temp_word_buffer);            //low byte
                uart_putc(temp_word_buffer>>8);         //high byte
                // increment address by 2, since it's a byte address
                flash_loc += 2;
    }}
    // if memory type is eeprom
    else if (memory_type == 'E'){
        uint16_t i;
        for (i = 0; i < buffer_size; i += 1) {
                uint8_t temp_buffer;
                // read and send byte
                temp_buffer = eeprom_read_byte((uint8_t *)eeprom_loc);
                uart_putc(temp_buffer);
                eeprom_loc++;
    }}
    else {uart_putc('?');}
    break;
default:   // default: respond with '?'
        uart_putc('?');
        break;
    }END**
```

Just as a point of clarification, at the end of the program you should have three '}'.

After you have saved your program run the 'make' command again, after correcting any errors we will move on. The complete bootloader.c source code follows, broken into sections for ease of displaying

BOOTLOADER.C source code

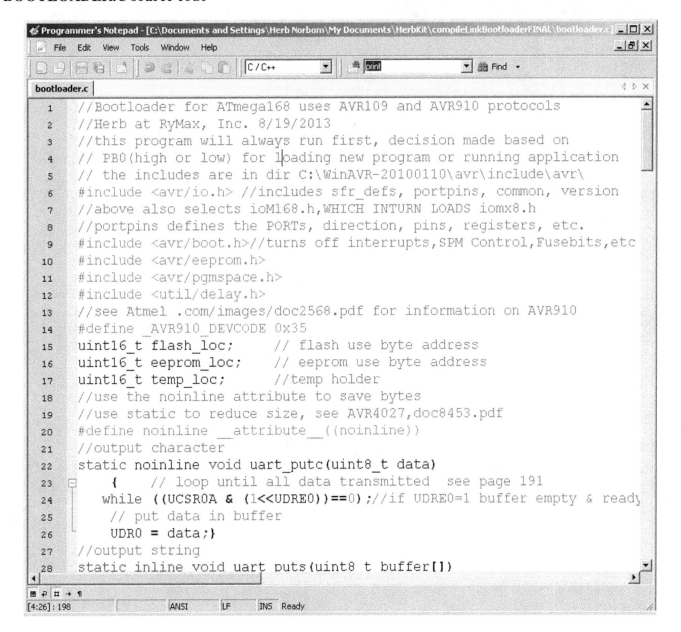

```
1   //Bootloader for ATmega168 uses AVR109 and AVR910 protocols
2   //Herb at RyMax, Inc. 8/19/2013
3   //this program will always run first, decision made based on
4   // PB0(high or low) for loading new program or running application
5   // the includes are in dir C:\WinAVR-20100110\avr\include\avr\
6   #include <avr/io.h> //includes sfr_defs, portpins, common, version
7   //above also selects ioM168.h,WHICH INTURN LOADS iomx8.h
8   //portpins defines the PORTs, direction, pins, registers, etc.
9   #include <avr/boot.h>//turns off interrupts,SPM Control,Fusebits,etc
10  #include <avr/eeprom.h>
11  #include <avr/pgmspace.h>
12  #include <util/delay.h>
13  //see Atmel .com/images/doc2568.pdf for information on AVR910
14  #define _AVR910_DEVCODE 0x35
15  uint16_t flash_loc;      // flash use byte address
16  uint16_t eeprom_loc;     // eeprom use byte address
17  uint16_t temp_loc;       //temp holder
18  //use the noinline attribute to save bytes
19  //use static to reduce size, see AVR4027,doc8453.pdf
20  #define noinline __attribute__((noinline))
21  //output character
22  static noinline void uart_putc(uint8_t data)
23      {    // loop until all data transmitted  see page 191
24    while ((UCSR0A & (1<<UDRE0))==0);//if UDRE0=1 buffer empty & ready
25    // put data in buffer
26    UDR0 = data;}
27  //output string
28  static inline void uart_puts(uint8_t buffer[])
```

Programmer's Notepad - [C:\Documents and Settings\Herb Norbom\My Documents\HerbKit\compileLinkBootloaderFINAL\bootloader.c]

File Edit View Tools Window Help

C / C++   print   Find

bootloader.c

```
29          {      // send until end of string
30      while (*buffer != 0) {
31          uart_putc(*buffer);
32          buffer++;}}
33  //read character
34   static noinline uint8_t uart_getc(void)
35      {     // wait for character to be received
36      while (!(UCSR0A & (1<<RXC0)));
37      /* return received byte */
38      return UDR0;}
39  //init the hardware uart
40   static inline void init_uart(void)
41      {     // set baud rate for 115,200 using F_CPU =14745600
42      UBRR0H = 0;
43      UBRR0L = 7;      //see page 198 set 115,200 baud
44      UCSR0B = (1<<RXEN0)|(1<<TXEN0);//enable Rec&Trans,pages192-193
45      UCSR0C = (1<<UCSZ01)|(1<<UCSZ00);} //see page194 set for 8 bit
46
47  int main(void){
48      uint8_t memory_type;
49      uint16_t buffer_size;
50      init_uart();
51      DDRB &= ~(1<<PB0);   //PORT DATA REGISTER set as input
52      PORTB |= (1<<PB0);   //PORT DATA REGISTER enable pullup
53      // wait a little
54      _delay_loop_1(200);
55      // bootloader test to see if new program to load
56      if(PINB == 0) {//if PINB is pulled to ground
```

[39:6] : 198   ANSI   LF   INS Ready

Programmer's Notepad - [C:\Documents and Settings\Herb Norbom\My Documents\HerbKit\compileLinkBootloaderFINAL\bootloader.c]

File   Edit   View   Tools   Window   Help

C / C++   print   Find

bootloader.c

```
57           goto start_bootloader;
58       } else { //start application
59  //DataSheet page65, jump to application program start of flash memory
60  // interrupt vector to start of flash, IVSEL
61           MCUCR = 0;
62           asm("jmp 0000");}
63  start_bootloader:     // main communication loop with avrdude
64       while (1)
65       {//commands from avrdude also look at AVR109 Protocol doc1644.pdf
66           uint8_t avrdude_cmd = uart_getc();
67           switch (avrdude_cmd){
68               case 'P':   //Enter Programming Mode
69                   uart_putc('\r');
70                   break;
71               case 'L':   //Leave Programming Mode
72                   uart_putc('\r');
73                   break;
74               case 'a':   //Auto Increment Address
75                   uart_putc('Y');
76                   break;
77               case 'A'://Start address, we want to start at byte 0,
78                       //but it looks like avrdude needs us to read
79                       //the address so read and ignore
80                   temp_loc = (uart_getc() << 8) | uart_getc();
81                   eeprom_loc = 0;      //set to zero
82                   flash_loc = 0;       //set to zero
83                   uart_putc('\r');
84                   break;
```

Bootloader Source Code for ATMega168 using STK500 for MS Windows   Page 25

Programmer's Notepad - [C:\Documents and Settings\Herb Norbom\My Documents\HerbKit\compileLinkBootloaderFINAL\bootloader.c]

File   Edit   View   Tools   Window   Help

C / C++   print   Find

bootloader.c

```
85              case 'e'://Chip Erase, all pages in flash, as per lock-bits
86                          //bootloader section should be protected by lock-bits
87                  for (flash_loc = 0; flash_loc < BOOT_SECTION_START;
88                      flash_loc += SPM_PAGESIZE) {
89                      boot_page_erase_safe(flash_loc);}
90                  uart_putc('\r');
91                  break;
92              case 'T':   // Select Device Type: received device type
93                  uart_getc();
94                  uart_putc('\r');
95                  break;
96              case 's'://Read Signature Bytes: send signature bytes for MCU
97                  uart_putc(SIGNATURE_2);//FROM iom168.h, Datasheet page289
98                  uart_putc(SIGNATURE_1);
99                  uart_putc(SIGNATURE_0);
100                 break;
101             case 't'://Return Supported Device Codes,terminate with nullbyte
102                 uart_putc(_AVR910_DEVCODE);
103                 uart_putc(0);
104                 break;
105             case 'S':   // Return Software Identifier, send s[7]
106                 uart_puts((uint8_t *)"RyMax");
107             case 'p':   // Return Programmer Type, 'S' for serial
108                 uart_putc('S');
109                 break;
110             case 'E':   // Exit Bootloader
111                 uart_putc('\r');
112                 break;
```

Programmer's Notepad - [C:\Documents and Settings\Herb Norbom\My Documents\HerbKit\compileLinkBootloaderFINAL\bootloader.c]

File   Edit   View   Tools   Window   Help

C / C++   print   Find

bootloader.c

```
113            case 'b': // Check Block Support: return yes,another byte,block size
114                uart_putc('Y');
115                uart_putc(0);
116                uart_putc(SPM_PAGESIZE);
117                break;
118            case 'B':    // Start Block Flash Load, read buffer size (in bytes)
119                buffer_size = (uart_getc() << 8) | uart_getc();
120                // check buffer size not exceeded
121                if (buffer_size > SPM_PAGESIZE) {
122                    uart_putc('?');
123                    break;}
124                //read flash ('F') or eeprom ('E') memory type
125                memory_type = uart_getc();
126                if (memory_type == 'F'){
127                    uint16_t i;
128                    uint16_t temp_word_buffer;
129                        if (flash_loc > BOOT_SECTION_START) {
130                            uart_putc(0);}
131                    uint16_t temp_address = flash_loc;
132                    boot_spm_busy_wait();
133                    // read data, wordwise, low byte first
134                    for (i = 0; i < buffer_size/2; i++) {
135                        // get data word
136                        temp_word_buffer = uart_getc() | (uart_getc() << 8);
137                        // write data to temporary buffer
138                        boot_page_fill(temp_address, temp_word_buffer);
139                        // increment by two, since temp_address is a byte
140                        // address, but we are writing words!
```

Bootloader Source Code for ATMega168 using STK500 for MS Windows   Page 27

Programmer's Notepad - [C:\Documents and Settings\Herb Norbom\My Documents\HerbKit\compileLinkBootloaderFINAL\bootloader.c]

File   Edit   View   Tools   Window   Help

C / C++   print   Find

bootloader.c

```
141                            temp_address += 2;}
142                     // after filling the temp buffer, write the page
143                     boot_page_write_safe(flash_loc);
144                     boot_spm_busy_wait();
145                     // re-enable application flash section for read
146                     boot_rww_enable();
147                     // store next page address, auto-address-incrementing
148                     flash_loc = temp_address;
149                     uart_putc('\r');
150                 }
151             else if (memory_type == 'E'){
152                 uint8_t temp_data;
153                 uint16_t i;
154                 for (i = 0; i < buffer_size; i++) {
155                     temp_data = uart_getc();
156                     eeprom_write_byte( (uint8_t *)eeprom_loc, temp_data);
157                         eeprom_loc++;}
158                 uart_putc('\r');
159                 }
160                 else {uart_putc('?');}
161                 break;
162         case 'g':   // Start Block Flash Read, read byte counter
163                 buffer_size = (uart_getc() << 8) | uart_getc();
164                 // then, read memory type
165                 memory_type = uart_getc();
166                 // memory type is flash
167                 if (memory_type == 'F')
168                     {   // read buffer_size words
```

Programmer's Notepad - [C:\Documents and Settings\Herb Norbom\My Documents\HerbKit\compileLinkBootloaderFINAL\bootloader.c]

File   Edit   View   Tools   Window   Help

C / C++   print   Find

bootloader.c

```
169        uint16_t i;
170        for (i = 0; i < buffer_size; i += 2) {
171            uint16_t temp_word_buffer;//define 16bit word size
172            // read word
173            temp_word_buffer = pgm_read_word(flash_loc);
174            // send data as word
175            uart_putc(temp_word_buffer);          //low byte
176            uart_putc(temp_word_buffer>>8);        //high byte
177            // increment address by 2, since it's a byte address
178            flash_loc += 2;
179        }}
180        // if memory type is eeprom
181        else if (memory_type == 'E'){
182            uint16_t i;
183            for (i = 0; i < buffer_size; i += 1) {
184                uint8_t temp_buffer;
185                // read and send byte
186                temp_buffer = eeprom_read_byte((uint8_t *)eeprom_loc);
187                uart_putc(temp_buffer);
188                eeprom_loc++;
189            }}
190        else {uart_putc('?');}
191        break;
192    default:    // default: respond with '?'
193        uart_putc('?');
194        break;
195  }   }   }
```

[192:53] : 198   ANSI   LF   INS   Ready

With our error free bootloader.c we are ready to work on our Makefile to load the program on to our microchip. I am going to write this Makefile in a separate directory. I think it is easier to keep everything straight. Change to the 'uploadBootloader' directory and open your text editor. We are going to define variables and use sections of the Makefile so we can run various parts of it. As I do not want to copy the hex file we need to load from our 'compileLinkBootloader' directory we are going to use a variable name that has the path and file name for the hex file we want to load. For the variable names you can of course use what you want, just be consistent. The ones I am using seem to fit the purpose of being somewhat self describing.

Makefile Upload bootloader.hex

Go ahead and key the file into your text editor. If you are using Programmer's Notepad save as a 'Make' use the file name 'Makefile'. Be sure to save it in the correct directory so you don't erase the other Makefile. We are going to use variable names because there is a lot of repeating going on in this file. For spacing on a new line use TAB and not spaces. Many of the editors handle this automatically to some extent.

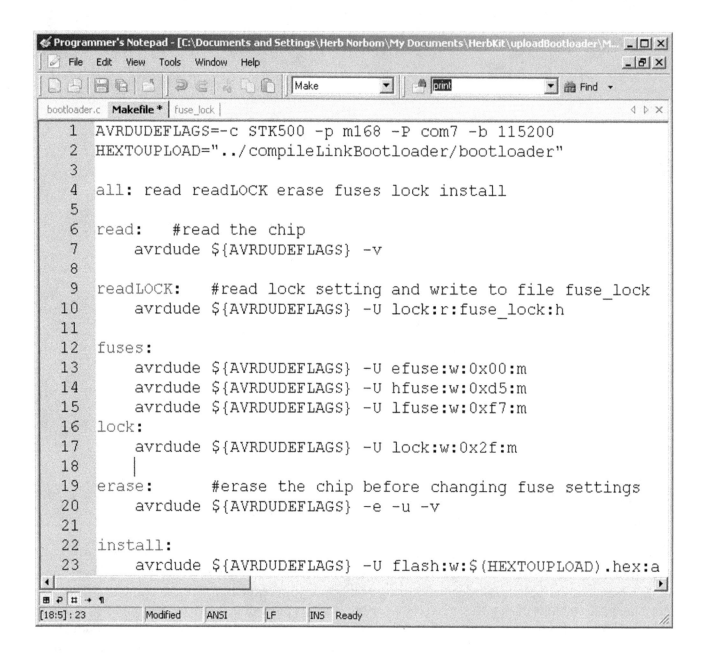

I suggest you follow the order shown in the following when running the Makefile. Put your chip on the breadboard, make sure pin1 in correct position. Have your STK500 hooked up to the USB port on the computer. You will need the external power to the breadboard 'on'. You will of course be running from the command prompt in our directory where we saved the new Makefile.

- make read   A simple read of your microchip to make sure all is working. This will execute the 'read' section only. Check the fuse hex values.

- make readlock   Read of the lock bits, and writes to file, check the file to make sure okay.

- make fuses   This will set your fuses. If you have them correct you can skip this step.

- make lock   This will set your lock bits. If you have them correct you can skip this step.

- make erase   This will erase the application section of the microchip's flash memory. As long as you have the lock bits set correctly it will not impact the 'BOOT_LOADER_SECTION. You always want to run erase prior to uploading a program.

- make install   This will install our bootloader.hex file on to the microchip.

Once you are feeling pretty good about all the actions taking place you can just type 'make' and all the sections of the Makefile will execute. You of course used a lot of the avrdude commands before when we were working with setting the fuses and lock bits.

BUILD YOUR LIBRARY

We will want to have modules, headers or programs that we can control and easily load into our programs. The WinAvr library is great, but we really don't want to mess around with it. At least I don't. One program that you can be pretty sure you will use is the UART serial communication. At least our test program will use it and you will get the idea of how to build your own library. Open your Programmer's Notepad or text editor and we will create a simple header file. In case you are wondering a header file is just a text file with a '.h' extension. We will create the 'uart.h' file, save it in 'herbClib'. The file type is 'C/C++'. The complete header is nine lines.

START**

```
#ifndef __UART_H
#define __UART_H

#include <inttypes.h>
#include <stdio.h>

FILE mystream;

void uart_init();

int uart_putchar(char x, FILE *stream);
int uart_getchar(FILE *stream);

#endif
```

END**

Next we want to write the uart.c program. This is very similar to what we wrote in the bootloader.c program.

I am just going to give you a complete program screen shot, as we covered just about all of the items before with the exception of writing to a FILE and *stream. For more information on that check your Datasheet, pages 180 – 191.

File   Edit   View   Tools   Window   Help

testAVRlib.c | uart.h | **uart.c** *

```
1    // uart.c Herb RyMax, Inc. greatly simplied, but just the basics
2    //remember the .h file is just made with an editor
3    // ATmega168 or ATmega328p, 14.7456 MHz clock
4    //page references are to ATmega168 Datasheet
5    #include <stdio.h>
6    #include <stdlib.h>
7    #include <avr/io.h>
8    #include <inttypes.h>
9    #include "uart.h"
10   void uart_init()
11   {
12       UBRR0H = 0;
13       UBRR0L = 7;      //see page 198 set 115,200 baud
14       UCSR0B = (1<<RXEN0) | (1<<TXEN0);  //enable Rec & Trans,page 193
15       UCSR0B |= (1<<RXCIE0); //enable uart RX RECEIVE Interrupt,page192
16       UCSR0C = (1<<UCSZ01) | (1<<UCSZ00); //see page 194 set for 8 bit
17   }
18   int uart_putchar(char c, FILE *stream) {  //see page 180 & 191
19       while ((UCSR0A & (1<<UDRE0))==0);   //if UDRE0=1 buffer empty
20                                            //and ready for new data
21           UDR0 = c;          // send keyboard input
22       return 0;
23   }
24   int uart_getchar(FILE *stream) {
25       char x = UDR0; //get data
26       return x;
27   }
```

[20:53] : 28   Modified   ANSI   LF   INS   Ready

Now that you have your uart.c program and uart.h header file ready we need to write a Makefile to compile into an output file 'uart.o'.

Enter the following and save as 'Makefile', type will be "Make" in the herbClib.

START**

#make file compiling uart.c for herbClib
all: uart.o
uart.o: uart.c
        @echo "Starting herbClib compile to build output 'o' file"
        avr-gcc -g -Os -Wall -mmcu=atmega168 -o uart.o -c uart.c
END**

After you have the Makefile completed, go ahead and type 'make' from the command prompt in the 'herbClib' directory.

This will produce the uart.o file. Once you are finished here proceed to the TEST PROGRAM section.

TEST PROGRAM

Now that we have our very own bootloader of course we want to write a program and upload it to our microchip. The purpose of this program is to test our library and see if we have communications with our PC. We will also define a pin for output and flash a LED. We will use a terminal communication program on the PC, for displaying information from the microchip and simple response back to the microchip from the PC. Two possible programs that you can use are 'PuTTY' or HyperTerminal. My examples are going to be shown using PuTTY. Another area that I want to touch on is eeprom memory. This is non-volatile memory that you can store data in. The data is retained when the power goes off. I am just going to write two simple integers to the eeprom, read them back and display them on the console. A little later I will cover reading eeprom using a 'dump' command in avrdude terminal mode.

testAVRlib.c

Complete source code shown using screen shots.

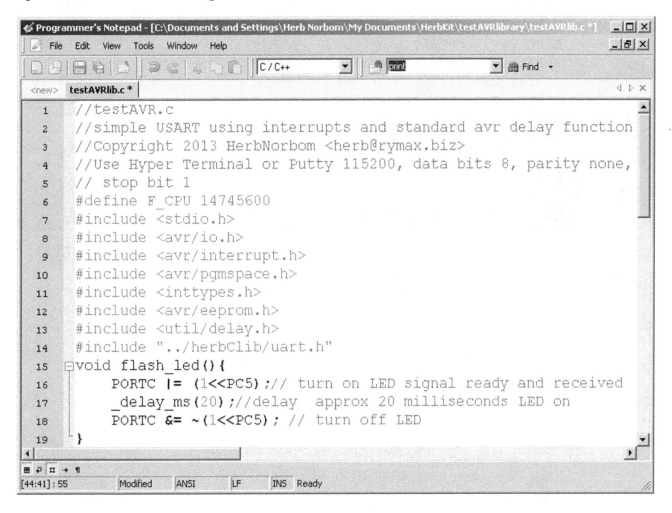

File Edit View Tools Window Help

`C / C++`   `print`   Find

`<new>`   **testAVRlib.c ***

```
20    ISR(USART_RX_vect)        // interrupt on USART
21        {
22        flash_led();           //signal data received
23        char ReceivedByte;
24        ReceivedByte = UDR0;
25        printf_P(PSTR("%c"),ReceivedByte);
26        if (ReceivedByte =='\r')
27            {printf_P(PSTR("\r\n line feed received \r\n"));}
28    }
29    int main()
30    {
31        DDRC |= (1<<PC5);
32        PORTC |= (1<<PC5);
33        _delay_ms(20);
34        PORTC &= ~(1<<PC5);
35        uart_init();    // start serial port  use for debugging
36        FILE uart_stream = FDEV_SETUP_STREAM(uart_putchar,
37            uart_getchar, _FDEV_SETUP_RW);
38        stdin = stdout = &uart_stream;
```

[44:41] : 55   Modified   ANSI   LF   INS   Ready

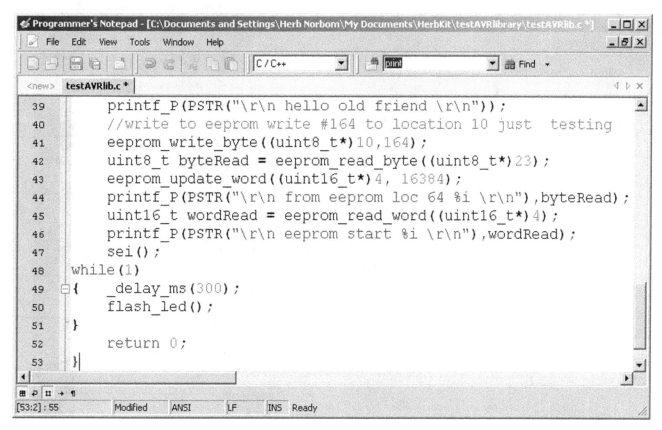

```
39      printf_P(PSTR("\r\n hello old friend \r\n"));
40      //write to eeprom write #164 to location 10 just  testing
41      eeprom_write_byte((uint8_t*)10,164);
42      uint8_t byteRead = eeprom_read_byte((uint8_t*)23);
43      eeprom_update_word((uint16_t*)4, 16384);
44      printf_P(PSTR("\r\n from eeprom loc 64 %i \r\n"),byteRead);
45      uint16_t wordRead = eeprom_read_word((uint16_t*)4);
46      printf_P(PSTR("\r\n eeprom start %i \r\n"),wordRead);
47      sei();
48  while(1)
49  {   _delay_ms(300);
50      flash_led();
51  }
52      return 0;
53  }
```

Application Breadboard

With our program written and saved we of course want to compile, link, assemble and upload to our Atmega168. To upload we are going to use our serial programer and not the STK500. You need a separate breadboard. As with our first breadboard I positioned the microchip so that pin 1 is in row 1 of the breadboard. The main difference is the communications, but there are other differences that I will detail.

The USB to TTL Serial Cable from Adafruit replaces the STK500 on the breadboard. The green wire of the serial cable will connect to PIN2, or the RXD pin. The white wire of the serial cable will connect to PIN3, or the TXD pin. The black wire of the serial cable will connect to the ground. The red wire of the serial cable can be connected to the red rail of the breadboard as it should be putting out 5v via the USB connection. I generally do not connect the red wire and rely on my external power source run through the voltage regulator. The choice is yours, my diagram will show an external power source.

I did not include a resistor on PC6 or PIN1 as we did on the previous breadboard.

As I want a flashing LED I ran a wire from PIN28, PC5 to breadboard row 20. I put a small resistor from row 20 to row 21. Then a small LED from row 21 to blue rail or ground. Remember which way your LED works. The long wire is for + (Anode) and the shorter leg or wire for – (Cathode). The short leg goes into the blue rail. The resistor is to limit current so the LED doesn't blow up or burn out to quickly. There are sites on web to help you do calculations. But do use a resistor.

We need a method to ground PIN14, you can use a switch as shown in the diagram or run a wire to the blue rail when you want to upload a program.

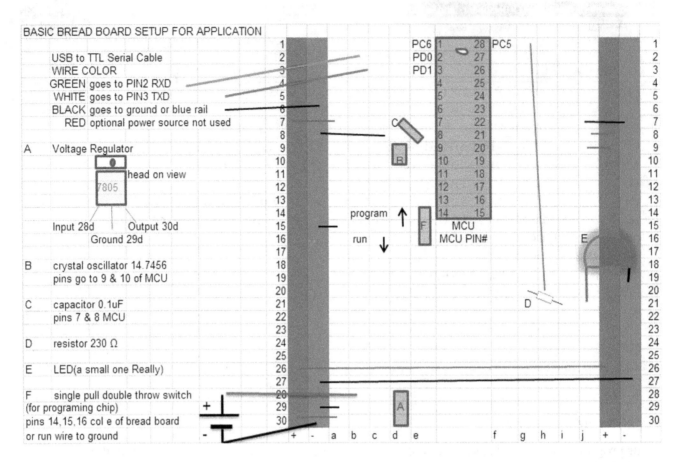

Compile Link Assemble Upload testAVRlib.c

We need one more Makefile. Using your Programmer's Notepad or other editor create and save the following with file name Makefile, type 'Make' in the same directory as your application program 'testAVRlib.c' in directory '..HerbKit\testAVRlibrary'. The complete Makefile is shown in the following along with a number of notes that you should not put in your Makefile.

Makefile content	DESCRIPTIONS DO NOT INCLUDE IN Makefile
# program name testAVRlib 8/23/2013	The # means this is a comment line.
# this is a simple Makefile to compile, link	
# assemble and upload the testAVRlib.hex file	
# to the ATMega168 microchip, Herb @ RyMax, Inc	
LINKFLAGS=-Wl,-u,vfprintf -lprintf_flt	Setup the options needed for linking in variable, easier to handle Linking, Wl (note this is a small letter L, not a '1'). Passing the item after the comma to the linker. What immediately follows the small l or linker command switch is the unique part of the library filename. The '-u' forces the items following to be entered in the output file as undefined. Triggers additional modules from the standand libraries. For outputing values to stream. Part of the c printf family. lprintf_flt allows for floating point. SEE \avr\include\stdio.h approx line 567 for more info.
LINKFLAGS+=-Wl,-u,vfscanf -lscanf_flt	For working with file stream.
LINKFLAGS+=-lm	Suboptions for linker, '-l' (small letter 'L') means include library name that immediately follows, an 'm' in our case. The 'm' is automatically expanded to the full name of 'libm.a' in our case. The file is located in C:\WinAvr-20100110\avr\lib\avr5 in our case.
LINKOBJECTS=../herbClib/uart.o	Setup the OBJECTS needed in variable, easier to handle
all: compile assemble upload	Define the sections
	If you get errors with the line continue put a space before it.
compile: testAVRlib.c	Section defined.
avr-gcc -g\	We are using the avr-gcc compilier, -g for producing debugging information. Note the '\' means the command continued on next line.
-Os\	Optimize for size.
-Wall\	Error warning level set to all
-mmcu=atmega168\	Specify the ATMEL AVR defined
$(LINKFLAGS)\	LINKER options see above
-o testAVRlib.o testAVRlib.c\	Write outpur to file, here testAVRlib.c output written to testAVRlib.o (Option use small letter o)
$(LINKOBJECTS)	see above
avr-objcopy -j .text -O ihex testAVRlib.o testAVRlib.hex	Copy the testAVRlib.o file to the testAVRlib.hex file and use the library to change to the desired format
assemble: testAVRlib.hex	Section defined.
avr-objdump -d testAVRlib.o > testAVRlib.ass	Information about the object file, testAVRlib.o is '-d' disassemble and build testAVRlib.ass file
upload: testAVRlib.hex	Section defined.
avrdude -c avr109\	Defining our programmer to avrdude
-p m168\	the AVR defined device we want to upload to
-P com2\	USB port our serial programmer is using
-b 115200\	Baud rate for serial programer
-U flash:(w):testAVRlib.hex:a	Memory operation, writing to flash memory our hex file

From your command prompt in the 'testAVRlibrary' directory you can run the Makefile in steps. For example 'make compile' to test compiling your program. When you are ready to upload your program to the microchip remember to set your switch to ground pin14. If you do not have a switch (F in diagram) you can run a wire to ground when you want to upload the application program. Disconnect the wire to run your application program. Turn on the auxiliary power to the breadboard.

When you are ready type 'make' at the command prompt, and you should see something similar to the following.

```
C:\WINDOWS\system32\cmd.exe                                    _|B|X|

C:\Documents and Settings\Herb Norbom\My Documents\HerbKit\testAVRlibrary>make
avr-gcc -g\
                -Os\
                -Wall\
                -mmcu=atmega168\
                -Wl,-u,vfprintf -lprintf_flt -Wl,-u,vfscanf -lscanf_flt -lm\
                -o testAVRlib.o testAVRlib.c \
                ../herbClib/uart.o
avr-objcopy -j .text -O ihex testAVRlib.o testAVRlib.hex
avr-objdump -d testAVRlib.o > testAVRlib.ass
avrdude -c avr109\
                -p m168\
                -P com2\
                -b 115200\
                -U flash:w:testAVRlib.hex:a

Connecting to programmer: .
Found programmer: Id = "       S"; type = S
    Software Version = ?. ; No Hardware Version given.
Programmer supports auto addr increment.
Programmer supports buffered memory access with buffersize=128 bytes.

Programmer supports the following devices:
    Device code: 0x35

avrdude: AVR device initialized and ready to accept instructions

Reading | ################################################## | 100% 0.00s

avrdude: Device signature = 0x1e9406
avrdude: NOTE: FLASH memory has been specified, an erase cycle will be performed

         To disable this feature, specify the -D option.
avrdude: erasing chip
avrdude: reading input file "testAVRlib.hex"
avrdude: input file testAVRlib.hex auto detected as Intel Hex
avrdude: writing flash (6784 bytes):

Writing | ################################################## | 100% 1.09s

avrdude: 6784 bytes of flash written
avrdude: verifying flash memory against testAVRlib.hex:
avrdude: load data flash data from input file testAVRlib.hex:
avrdude: input file testAVRlib.hex auto detected as Intel Hex
avrdude: input file testAVRlib.hex contains 6784 bytes
avrdude: reading on-chip flash data:

Reading | ################################################## | 100% 0.86s


avrdude: verifying ...
avrdude: 6784 bytes of flash verified

avrdude done.  Thank you.
```

Run Your Application Software

With a successful upload you are ready to run your software. Turn off the auxiliary power. Throw the switch to the 'run' position on your breadboard or disconnect the wire if you went that route. Open PuTTY with the following settings, serial, COM2(or your port), Speed=115200, Data bits =8, Stop bits =1, Parity =None, Flow control = None. Turn the auxiliary power back on and you should see the LED flashing and a message displayed on the PuTTY screen similar to the following.

As you can see we have our text message. If you type on the keyboard you should see your input on the PuTTY display, when you press return it should give you the message 'line feed received'. The last topic I want to touch on is reading the eeprom using avrdude in terminal mode.

Avrdude Terminal Mode Read eeprom

I have moved the microchip back to the STK500. With the auxiliary power on, enter the following from the command prompt to enter terminal mode: avrdude -c STK500 -p m168 -P com7 -t

Once you are in terminal mode enter the following after the 'avrdude.>' prompt to read a small portion of the eeprom:.

 dump eeprom 0 100

You should get a screen similar to the following.

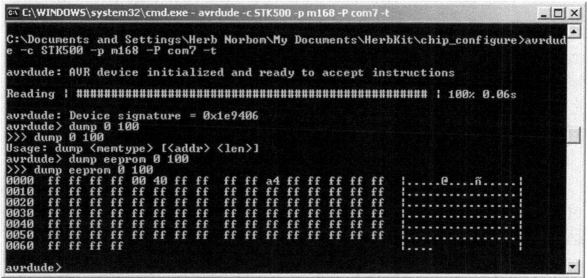

Reading the memory or should I say translating it is not too bad, just remember it is encoded. Back in our application program 'testAVRlib.c' on line 41 we wrote the number 164 to position 10 of eeprom. In the preceding display you can see 'a4' in memory location 10. (The first 'ff' is position 0 when counting). If you convert the 'a4' from hex to decimal you see our number 164. If you look at the right side of the display you see a translation from hex to character. The hex value 40 translates to the character '@'. The hex value a4 translates to 164, using the extended ASCII code we see the value as 'ñ'.

Our second write from our program was to memory address 4 and the value was 16384. This is a little more complicated. In memory location 4 we see '00' which tells us the next value (which is also hex) is to be multiplied by 256. First step, the hex value 40 is 64 in decimal. Second step multiply 64 by 256 which gives us 16384. But what if we had but 16385 as input to our program. Here we see that memory location 4 has

'01' which means we do as before but add one to the result of 64 * 256. See the following example.

To exit avrdude terminal mode type 'quit' or ctrl +z. If you have problems with uploading programs to your chip due to "avrdude: verification error; content mismatch" consider that we have set the HFuse to be preserved through a chip erase. You may want to try setting the HFuse hex to dd. That is just changing one value, the EESAVE from a 0 to a 1. This will permit erasing of the eeprom memory.

THE END OR THE BEGINNING
I hope that you have learned a lot and had some fun.

Visit the web site www.rymax.biz for additional information. I would like to learn from your experience, you can e-mail me at herb@rymax.biz.

APPENDIX

Simple DOS commands

For those who may have forgotten some simple DOS commands, a very quick refresher course follows. I am going to create a directory in the location where my 'cmd' prompt opened. Adjust the following as needed for your system. Before we go any further, a few quick words on DOS commands. They can do damage, they are not very user friendly; they will destroy without asking twice. So make sure the command you enter is the command that you want and that you know what the command is going to do.

Simple DOS commands, execute from the DOS command prompt. Remember DOS is not case sensitive.

- Dir or dir – This will give you the contents of the current directory
- Help – all the commands that are available
- Help dir – gives you all the options available with dir
- cd {dir name}– change directory, you would add the directory name
- cd ../ – moves up the directory tree one level
- cls –clear the DOS window screen

To create a directory to store our programs. Call the directory 'HerbKit'.

mkdir HerbKit –this will create the directory

To see if the directory was created type 'dir herb*' this should list your work directory and any other file or directory starting with 'w' the * is called a wild card.

Bit Manipulation

If you are not familiar with bit manipulation you need to work on understanding this. In the following we will just touch on the subject. Some of the Bitwise Operators are shown in the following table.

Operator	Meaning	Description
&	AND	For combining bytes, both bits must be a 1 to move a 1 to the result. If either bit is a 0 the result will be a 0.
|	OR	For combining bytes, if either bit = 1 then the resulting bit will be a 1.
^	XOR	Bitwise exclusive or. Look at two bytes and compare each bit position. If both bits are a 1 the result is 0. If either bit is a 1 result is a 1. If both bits are 0, result is 0.
>>1	RIGHT SHIFT	Shift all the bits in the byte to the RIGHT and fill vacated bit with a 0.
>>3		Shift all the bits in the byte to the RIGHT 3 positions and fill vacated bits with a 0.
<<1	LEFT SHIFT	Shift all the bits in the byte to the LEFT and fill vacated bit with a 0.
<<3		Shift all the bits in the byte to the LEFT 3 positions and fill vacated bits with a 0.
~	TILDE	Flips every bit in the byte, a 1 becomes a 0 and a 0 becomes a 1.

To clarify some examples, the first table will show the decimal values with corresponding binary value as they are assigned to the byte. In the second table we will perform the operations and show the resulting binary and decimal values. The 'Ref' is like a variable or register name. Also, just to add some additional clarification including the hex values.

REF	DECIMAL	7	6	5	4	3	2	1	0	HEX VALUE
A	0	0	0	0	0	0	0	0	0	0
B	1	0	0	0	0	0	0	0	1	1
C	2	0	0	0	0	0	0	1	0	2
D	3	0	0	0	0	0	0	1	1	3
E	4	0	0	0	0	0	1	0	0	4
F	5	0	0	0	0	0	1	0	1	5
G	6	0	0	0	0	0	1	1	0	6
H	7	0	0	0	0	0	1	1	1	7
I	8	0	0	0	0	1	0	0	0	8
J	9	0	0	0	0	1	0	0	1	9
K	10	0	0	0	0	1	0	1	0	A

Simple examples using the above Reference variables. Where the same Reference variable is referenced go to first table and assume value not changed by the example.

Operations	7	6	5	4	3	2	1	0	DECIMAL VALUE	HEX VALUE
A&B	0	0	0	0	0	0	0	0	0	0
A|B	0	0	0	0	0	0	0	1	1	1
G&H	0	0	0	0	0	1	1	0	6	6
G|H	0	0	0	0	0	1	1	1	7	7
K>>1	0	0	0	0	0	1	0	1	5	5
K<<1	0	0	0	1	0	1	0	0	20	14

PuTTY

For our communications you will need PuTTY© or some other terminal interface program. If you do not have one I suggest you try PuTTY. The following describes how to obtain the PuTTY executable. Go to the main PuTTY Download Page. http://www.chiark.greenend.org.uk/~sgtatham/putty/download.html. From this page you can select the appropriate file. I suggest you get the Windows installer for everything except PuTTYtel. At this point the latest release is version .63.

Open PuTTY and click on Serial, make appropriate changes. I am setting up for baud of 115200, as this speed is what I plan to use in our test program. Also I have set Flow control to 'None'. The PuTTY help files should have been included if things are not working.

HyperTerminal

With HyperTerminal you will go through something similar to PuTTY but of course very different. On the NerdKit web site under the 'servo squirter' tutorial, there is a good discussion on HyperTerminal. If you have HyperTerminal it can generally be found from the Start window, All Programs, Accessories, and Communications. Suggest you create a shortcut and paste to your desktop.

Geany For Windows

The program has many useful features as well as being a very nice text editor. Go to www.geany.org . The geany-1.2.3.1 setup.exe Full Installer is approximately 8Mb. This has some nice features for configuration of Makefile and uploading the program.

www.ingramcontent.com/pod-product-compliance
Lightning Source LLC
Chambersburg PA
CBHW060511060326
40689CB00020B/4698